CLERGY AND VICTIMS
OF

VIOLENT
CRIME

PREPARING FOR CRISIS COUNSELING

DR. WAYNE LEAVER

C.S.S. Publishing Co., Inc.
Lima, Ohio

BV
4339
.L42
1990

Copyright © 1990 by
The C.S.S. Publishing Company, Inc.
Lima, Ohio

Library of Congress Cataloging-in-Publication Data

Leaver, Wayne, 1947-
    Clergy and victims of violent crime: preparing for crisis counseling / by Wayne Leaver.
        p.   cm.
    Developed from the content of several workshops sponsored by the Miami Chapter of Parents of Murdered Children and held in 1988.
    Includes bibliographical references (p.).
    ISBN 1-55673-203-1
    1. Victims of Crime — Pastoral counseling of.   2. Violent crimes.
I. Title.
BV4339.L42   1990
253.5--dc20
                                                                                        86-28577
                                                                                        CIP

9022 / ISBN 1-55673-203-1   PRINTED IN U.S.A.

Dedicated

To the members of
Parents of Murdered Children, Miami Chapter,
who have worked to help others
at a time of violent death.

— and —

To Edie Stark,
Death Educator and Grief Counselor,
who has given of herself
in helping Parents of Murdered Children.

Contents

Introduction

The content of this book comes out of several workshops for clergy sponsored by the Parents of Murdered Children of the Miami, Florida Chapter held in 1988. These workshops were co-sponsored by the Miami District of the United Methodist Church; the Episcopal Diocese of Southeast Florida; the Christian Community Service Agency's Family Counseling Center; the Jackson Memorial Hospital Chaplain Services; the Miami Urban Ministries of the United Methodist Church; the Union for Experimenting Colleges and Universities, Miami Center; the Rabbinical Association Service; Mothers Against Drunk Driving, Miami Chapter; the Catholic Archdiocese of Miami; the Family Enrichment Center of the Archdiocese of Miami; the Miami Baptist Association; and the Anthony Abraham Foundation.

Among the key presenters were Sara Arnwine, President of Parents of Murdered Children, Miami Chapter; Edie Stark, Death Educator and Grief Counselor; Janet Reno, State Attorney for Dade County, Florida; Rev. Dr. Wayne Leaver, pastor of Coral Way — Southwest United Methodist Churches and Dean of the Union for Experimenting Colleges and Universities, Miami Center; and the Rev. Donald Norris, pastor of South Miami Baptist Church and Chaplain at Jackson Memorial Hospital.

The reading lists and handouts were put together by Edie Stark. It is upon many of these materials that the content of this book is based. However, no one but the author should be held accountable for the content of this book.

It is our hope that this volume will introduce clergy to the needs of victims and to the essential elements in ministering to families when violent crime strikes.

Chapter One

The Rise of Violent Death and the Need for Ministry

It u;ed to be that violent crime seldom involved people in our churches or synagoges. It was said, "Our people are good people and crime is something that happens to bad people." If it did happen to our "good people," we were able to convince ourselves that it was something out of the ordinary. Our seminary training may have included general grief counseling and how to conduct funerals, but nothing was ever said about violent death or how to minister to families who were victims of violent crime.

These simplistic attitudes have proven inadequate in today's world. What happened? According to Marion Harris in his book *America Now: The Anthropology of a Changing Culture,* the F.B.I. Uniform Crime Report between 1945 and 1975 shows robberies in the U.S. increased 500 percent, and between 1975 and 1980 the rate of violent crime in the U.S. (murder, rape, and robbery) increased 250 percent. He points out that there are 20,000 homicides a year in the United States. The United States has seven times more homicides than Great Britain, twelve times more rapes, and eight times more robberies. The United States has five times more homicides than Japan, ten times more rapes, and seventeen times more robberies.[1] We are a violent culture.

And the rate of violent crime has greatly increased. It is not just the drug dealers or other criminals who are getting killed, but "good people," too. We in the clergy cannot avoid ministering to families who have been victims of violent crime.

In fact, it appears that things may get worse before they get better. The Justice Department's study (based on figures compiled by the government's National Crime Survey from 1975 through 1984) states that five out of six of today's twelve-year-olds will be the victims or intended victims of violent crime during their lifetimes if current crime rates persist. Half of them will be victimized more than once. Nearly one out of twelve females will be the victim of an attempted or completed rape. It said that forty-five percent of black males, twenty-four percent of black females, thirteen percent of white females, and thirty-seven percent of white males will be victims of violent crime. It is young people who are most likely to be victims. An estimated seventy-two percent of the nation's twenty-year-olds, fifty-three percent of thirty-year-olds, twenty-two percent of fifty-year-olds, fourteen percent of sixty-year-olds, and eight percent of seventy-year-olds are expected to be victims of violent crime. [2]

My own community of Dade County, Florida, in 1986 had the highest killing rate and highest rate of major crimes among metropolitan areas on the U.S. mainland, according to the F.B.I Uniform Crime Report. In 1988 the Dade County Medical Examiner's Office reported 488 homicides, down from 621 in 1981. [3] In 1988, 153 police officers lost their lives in the line of duty nationwide. California lost twenty-three, Texas twenty-one, and Florida thirteen. In 1988, one officer died every fifty-seven hours. One household in four suffered at least one crime of violence or theft — a total of more than twenty-two million households. The chance of being a violent crime victim is greater than that of being hurt in a traffic accident. Criminal homicide is one of the fifteen most frequent causes of death, and for the fifteen- to thirty-nine-year-old group, it is second only to accidents as a cause of death. [4]

As you can see, violent crime is a major problem in the United States. Odds are that you may be one of the victims during your lifetime.

There is a tremendous need for the community to address this problem. The causes of crime need to be explored, identified, and addressed. The screening, training, and supporting of police are important issues. The inadequacy and injustice of th riminal justice system are a disgrace. The rights of victims eed to be affirmed — even as the rights of the accused and e prisoners have been affirmed. "Truth in sentencing," ov rowded jails, lack of needed prisons, parole systems, a of the concept of gain or good time, and the issue of r oilitation — all are demanding the public's attention.

As clergy, many of us are involved in prison ministries and -way house ministries. There is also a need for ministry n the victims and families of victims of violent crime. The ception is that clergy are concerned for those who commit e crimes, but not the victims. In a recent widely publicized urder in Miami, the cleric discovered that both the victim nd murderer were members of his particular congregation. Jnfortunately, he spent the first couple days with the family)f the murderer and was surprised at the reaction he received when he got around to visiting the family of the victim. In another recent case in Miami, the Archbishop spoke in court for the murderer of a man because he had been an altar boy — the victim had been an altar boy, too.

We clergy are not always aware of the image and message we send by our acts. This short introductory book is a call to minister to the victims and their families. Its aim is to help clergy to understand the peculiar grief process that victims must endure, and the special problems presented by the criminal justice system to the grief process. It contains practical advice and suggestions on what to do and what not to do in ministering to victims. Increasingly, victims will be members of our congregation of faith. We need to prepare ourselves.

Endnotes

1. Harris, Marion, *American Now,* New York: Simon and Schuster, 1981. pp. 118-119.

2. *The Miami Herald*, March 9th, 1987, p. A 4.

3. *The Miami Herald*, July 28, 1987, p. B 1.

4. Research Program Plan, Fiscal year 1989, National Institute of Justice, November 1988, p. 31.

Chapter Two

The First Forty-Eight Hours

T he following are statements by those who have lived those terrible forty-eight hours:

It was so unreal. It didn't seem possible. I thought it was a bad dream, a nightmare. I guess I was in shock. They didn't want me to see his body. But I had to be sure it was him. Only then could I believe he was dead.
— *a mother*

I don't really remember what was said or what happened after they told us. I must have blocked it all out. — *a father*

My daughter Stacy was ten years old. She was murdered two weeks before her birthday. I had just lost my wife to cancer four months earlier after a lengthy illness. . . . I had left Stacy home that day; she wasn't feeling good. . . . I walked into the house. I noticed a light on in her room. I walked into her room and found her. She was lying on the bed and it was a blood bath. I got a neighbor. He came into the house. We called the police. An ambulance was called. In the midst of this bedlam the police took me downtown. Before I knew it they were accusing me of the murder. They took mug shots. They did everything but actually book me for the murder. The trauma I went through that night finding my daughter — and just getting over my wife's death — and I come in and find my daughter butchered and in the next couple of hours I am accused by the police. They are just assuming I did it and they are telling me all kinds of things, that my daughter and I were having sex. They found out from a neighbor of mine that I had told him that after my wife died, my daughter had wanted to sleep in my room. She was afraid to be alone. They turned it around and tried to use it to

imply that I was sleeping with her on a sexual level. If you can imagine the horror I was going through that night. It was beyond belief. Even to this day I have flashbacks about it. . . . I have to live with the fact that I found her, that I left her to get a job that day that I needed in the worst way. All those things I had to go through, the accusation that I did it to her. It was very traumatic.
— a father

The call to respond to families who have been the victims of a violent crime may come at any time. Clergy may encounter the victim's family in several possible settings. Each circumstance will be different. You may be asked to go with a police representative to notify the family at their home. You may be called to the hospital emergency room where the family has come upon notification of the violent event. You may be called to the scene of the crime, particularly if it is the victim's and family's home. You may not encounter the family until after they have been notified of the violent death, and a day or two have passed.

There is some basic information that clergy need to know and keep in mind when first responding to the family in such a crisis.

A sudden death often hits family survivors with a feeling of unreality. They simply cannot believe that such a thing has happened. They cannot believe it has happened to them, and to someone they love. When a sudden and violent death occurs, there has been no time to prepare. Survivors will tend to experience a longer period of shock and denial. Psychologically, this is the person's defense system acting normally to give them time to comprehend what has happened. Initial shock and denial gives the person time to accept what has happened without overloading their system. The clergy can best minister in this situation by physically being there for the survivors. Clergy should not reinforce the grieving person's denials. Nor is it appropriate to try to force the grieving person to give up their denial, as they will do so when they can.

There are times when a person's grief will lead them to excited physical actions. People will pound their fists, hit at doors and walls, walk and run, often trying to enter the surgical area to see their loved one. Clergy should restrain the angry griever only to protect the griever or others nearby. Unnecessary restraint only adds to the griever's sense of helplessness and anger.

Clergy can help grievers by giving permission for them to cry and let their grief out. The pain and grief will come out eventually, and now is an appropriate time to let it out. People around the survivors expect expressions of grief now, but if the grief is repressed and comes out weeks or months later, people around the survivors are not always accepting of those expressions. Because of religious beliefs in life after death, some people are reluctant to express their sense of loss and pain when a person dies. Clergy are able to help the grief process in people by giving permission for them to grieve and to mourn.

Clergy may encounter a strong sense of guilt on the part of survivors. It is not uncommon to hear a person say, "If only I had gone to the store instead of allowing her to go," "If only I had insisted that she learn self-defense or carry a gun," or "I should never have allowed him to be around those people." At first, many of these statements may sound valid. However, few people can foresee the future. Even if those actions had been taken, there is no guarantee that what happened would have been avoided. Often, survivors feel that, if only they had been there, they could have prevented the tragedy. At this early point of ministry with the survivors, clergy should avoid attacking or supporting these "if only . . ." beliefs. Instead, clergy need to continue giving support by physically being with the person and by continuing to give clear, concise information and reality orientation.

Closely related to a survivor's sense of guilt is often a need to blame someone else. In the case of a homicide, the murderer may or may not be known. Clergy must avoid the temptation to talk about "forgiving" the murderer. Such talk on the part of clergy is very close to falling back into cliches. The grieving person is not able to hear such concepts at this point of grief. To talk about forgiving the murderer now is to be totally insensitive to the grief process and the survivor's needs. This is really an effort by clergy to deal with their own needs. Clergy often feel the need to be the religious authority, and to promote the end results of their understanding of faith. Clergy must avoid falling into the "role" of a religious authority, and instead concentrate on being a caregiver. Clergy's anxiety in such a situation is understandable. But, at this point of encounter, clergy must help meet the needs of the grief sufferers instead of dealing with his or her own needs. Later in this book we will address the needs and feelings of clergy in ministering to victims of violent crime.

Clergy will usually confront the issue of the survivors viewing the loved one's body. Because of religious views held by many that the person's spirit, their soul, is no longer in the body, there is a tendency of the clergy to discourage viewing of the body. In the case of violent death, there is added concern about the condition of the body. The survivors may see injuries on the victim's body, think of the injuries the victim received, and be hurt and saddened even more. But seeing these injuries may also allow the survivors to feel a sense of relief that death freed the victim from the pain. Clergy can verbalize permission to view the body. This encourages reality orientation for the survivors. Some may still not really believe their loved one is dead. Clergy need to provide clear, concise communication to the survivors, for this is one of their greatest needs in time of shock. Clergy place a greater emphasis on the human spiritual and grieving needs of survivors by giving permission to view the body, than they do by trying to give spiritual explanations about the relationship of soul and body. The time for the theological explanations comes much later in the grief process. Clergy should show acceptance of the victim's body. This can be done by touching the body. This may allow the survivors a chance to say "good-bye" in the physical way, such as by a kiss. These situations are not easy for family or clergy. In my own experience, holding the body of a two-year-old child and talking to the mother and father as they held their son for the last time was one of the more difficult acts of ministry I have performed. Later, the family told me what a great comfort it was to them to say good-bye to their son in this way, and for me to be part of that experience with them.

At the time of viewing the body, clergy can continue reality orientation by helping the family to get clear communication about what happened. Because of the shock and feelings of unreality, families may need to ask many questions to clarify any misunderstandings. Clergy can help in this process, as doctors and nurses may be too busy or reluctant to get involved. The same may be true of any police who are present.

Sudden and violent deaths are frequently complicated by the involvement of medical and legal authorities. Issues of evidence gathering and legal determination of death may impede the family's opportunity to view or touch the body. It is important not to violate restrictions set by the police or medical officers. However, one should ascertain what is really required in the situation and help the medical and police authorities to see the needs of the survivors. Families want to know what will happen to their loved one's body. Clergy can help insure that families get these important questions answered directly by legal and medical officials. These answers play a part in determining funeral arrangements and can, sometimes, delay the funeral date. Autopsies, when a violent death has occurred, usually do not require the permission of the family.

Because the death is a homicide, or a death under violent conditions, investigators may well ask many questions of the survivors. Clergy may be tempted to intervene in an attempt to protect the family. However, these questions may be helpful in the long run in terms of understanding the causes of the death. The questions may also play a role in reality orientation for the survivors. The fact that the death is a matter of public record, and may appear in the newspaper or on television, is usually seen as an invasion of privacy. This is but one more factor involved with a violent death.

As clergy minister to survivors of violent crime, it is important as part of reality orientation that clergy use words such as "death" and "died." In their sorrow and shock, people have been known to interpret words like "passed on," "crossed the river," and the like to deny their loved one's death. Postponing acknowledgment of the death delays the grief process. Clergy must be supportive caregivers, but must also avoid being unwitting players in a grieving person's fantasy.

Medical staff will often offer sleeping pills and tranquilizers to the victim's family in an effort to help them through their ordeal. Clergy can intervene with the staff, or with the survivors, and raise questions as to whether this is a good course of action. Pills and caffeine block aspects of the grief process. As an alternative, juice, broth, herbal teas, or even a warm wrap can be used. Short term, mild tranquilizers may be appropriate for those with heart or blood pressure problems.

Clergy can help survivors by communicating in words and behaviors that anger and numbness are acceptable. Helping survivors understand that what they are feeling is all right and "normal" is reassuring, because some people will feel like they are "losing their minds." Clergy should avoid telling people to "get hold of themselves," or allow such messages to be accepted by the survivors. Instead, helping the survivors to be patient with themselves and not to build unrealistic expectations for their feelings and behavior can be helpful. The kind of care that needs to be provided might be called "regressive care." It surrounds the person with warmth and love, and is accepting and supporting. It is not a demanding love, demanding no heroic or stoic actions or attitudes. In some ways, it is like the care a mother gives to a very young child.

Being present, wholly present, for another person is a difficult task. As clergy, we want to help. We usually think that to help we have to do something. But it is important that we learn to be with the grieving person, rather than trying to solve the problem. Being present, sympathizing, suffering with, and understanding the other person is the connection for uplifting the person. We cannot make things better, and we cannot take away their pain. But, we can enter into it and share it with them.

As clergy, we must learn how to listen not only to the content of the words or message, but to the person's feelings and emotions. The temptation in many clergy is to respond intellectually to the content, while what is most needed in the first forty-eight hours is to hear and be sensitive to the person's feelings and emotions.

Once we hear what the person is communicating, we need to respond rather than simply react. We must not react only with our own feelings, but we must respond to the other person with understanding. We choose how we respond. Reacting is something we do uncritically and without thinking. Therefore, we must be aware of our own feelings, which may include reminders about previous or unsettled feelings in ourselves concerning deaths of loved ones. We must also be aware of our own feelings about our own death. We must choose to respond to the other person's needs, not to our own, and we must choose an appropriate response that does not deny or short-circuit the grief process.

We need to know ourselves, to realize that the revulsion or negative feelings we feel may be due to something within us that we are unwilling to accept about ourselves.

Behavior we find objectionable in others can signal that a defense mechanism is at work in us, or them, or both. Remembering that defense mechanisms are used by the ego to protect itself from real or imagined threats can help free us to accept the person behind the behavior. What appears to be an attack on us may be a defensive action on their part.

Being with another person at a time like this, should not involve minimizing their feelings or trying to cheer them up. Cheering them up is a form of discounting their feelings, instead of accepting them. Usually, we cheer people up so we can excuse ourselves and leave with a good conscience. Being with a person is not being nice. Being nice is often a form of discounting their behavior or not taking seriously the irritating and demanding behavior that masks their pain.

It is only by accepting our own pain, sin, and blindness that we can begin to accept others. Being wholly with another person is not just a matter of technique, but of being. We become a being more capable of doing this as we grow from our experiences.

The role of clergy in the first forty-eight hours is not that of a theologian or answer giver. Clergy must avoid cliches and the tendency to deal with their own anxiety by trying to hurry a person through the grief process. Instead, the clergy role is that of caregiver. It is to be physically and emotionally there as a spiritual ministry for the person in grief. While most clergy have been trained as reactors or responders to people, we may need to develop a more active, intervening role. People in shock and grief during the first forty-eight hours cannot be expected to think or act clearly. They cannot reasonably be expected to know what they need.

While our actions should be designed to give them as much control as possible, clergy need to take the initiative in ministering to survivors. Most basic of all is to be there physically for them. Clergy who say, "If you need me, call me," in situations like this, will not get calls. Instead, to be in ministry means to take the initiative in caregiving to the survivors of violent crime.

Clergy need to keep the initiative, because victims of violent crime may experience a sense of shock and unreality. They need the clergy to help in reality orientation. Survivors experience frustration in trying to find out and make sense of what has happened. Clergy can help provide clear, concise communication. Survivors experience pain. The emotions related may include anger, rage, depression, loss of control, loss of self-esteem, loss of purpose and meaning, loneliness, guilt, regret, and sadness. Suicidal tendencies and suicidal thoughts are not uncommon. Clergy need to provide regressive care of warm, accepting, supporting love. The basic way of doing this is to be there in solidarity with them. Your presence is much more important than your words. No one expects the clergy to make things better by saying a few words. Whatever you do or say can hardly make it worse. After all, someone they love has been suddenly and violently killed. Your time and effort help them to adjust to the loss of their loved one.

Clergy can also serve to begin the process of bringing others to surround the survivors in their loss. If family is not present with the survivors, you can inquire about who may be nearby, or who else might be contacted. Family members will usually come together to help each other. However, you may discover that the survivor has no family, or that family are ill, elderly, or live too far away to come in the near future. This is certainly a time to activate other caregivers in your church or religious group.The clergy person should be a direct caregiver and a coordinator of caregivers in such situations. Human solidarity and support is crucial for the survivors.

The Funeral

I suspected my daughter's husband of killing her. The funeral was in their home town where he grew up and where his family had influence. His family arranged the funeral and selected the minister. The minister never spoke to us concerning our feelings, or what we wanted.   — *a father*

Various religious traditions give guidance for the conduct of funeral or memorial services. Emotionally, the funeral is a benchmark for families in the grief process. It is a time of saying "good-byes." It is a formal and appropriate way of commemorating the deceased, and assigning the body to its resting place. Cremations and memorial services function in similar ways.

Theologically, clergy, depending upon their religious tradition, reflect upon death and the circumstances of death. One's religious views of life after death are expressed, and comfort from the Scriptures is offered.

Survivors' Emotional Experiences

- Sense of unreality
- Anger
- Guilt
- Sadness
- Loneliness
- Depression
- Rage
- Sense of violation
- Loss of self-esteem
- Loss of purpose & meaning
- Frustration
- Regret
- Sense of powerlessness
- Loss of control
- Suicidal thoughts & tendencies

Survivors' Needs

- Clear concise communication
- Reality orientation
- Experience of pain and loss
- Regressive care
- Solidarity with you and other family members

Clergy Don'ts

- Don't wait for an invitation to minister and give care.
- Don't use cliches.
- Don't try to give theological explanations in the first forty-eight hours.
- Don't join in the survivors' denials into talking about forgiving the murderer when they don't even know what happened.
- Don't downplay survivors' sense of guilt or neglect by dismissing these concerns casually.
- Don't encourage the use of pills or caffeine to get survivors through the ordeal.
- Don't tell survivors to "get hold of themselves," "bear it like a man," or any other stoic type of response.

Forty-Eight Hours

Clergy Don'ts (continued)

- Be aware of common temptations that have more to do with your fears and worries than those of the persons who have experienced the homicide in their family, namely:
  - our need to be in control of the situation
  - our own fear of violent death and fears for our family
  - the desire to "get in and get out" quickly
  - the use of platitudes or theologizing with easy answers, etc.

Clergy Do's

- Take the initiative and give care, minister.
- Give grieving persons permission to cry and express their grief.
- Verbalize permission to view the body.
- Clarify any misunderstandings about what occurred.
- Use words like "dead" and "died."
- Give clear and concise communication.
- Give regressive, warm, loving, accepting care.
- Be there physically for the griever.
- Help the person in grief understand that what they are feeling is "normal."
- Help the person in grief avoid unrealistic expectations of attitudes or actions.
- Restrain angry grieving persons only to protect them.
- Be aware of the general grief process.
- Be aware of your own anxieties, and don't confuse your needs with the grieving person's needs.
- Help the medical staff avoid "tranquilizing" the survivors.
- Help the survivors understand what happens next to the victim's body.
- Help mobilize family/church caregivers to be with the survivors.

For clergy, the difficult part in the liturgy is what to say about the deceased. The obtaining of this information can be a positive help to the family in grief. Clergy should always meet with the family well before the funeral to obtain this information. Since re-marriages are more common today, clergy need to be careful to involve as much of the family as possible. If people are coming in from out of town, special efforts may be needed to be sure that no one is left out. Clergy must be sensitive to family stresses and fissures. For relatives and loved ones to talk about the deceased can be a positive step for them in activating old memories and remembering the deceased in a positive way. Such experiences help them to organize their thoughts and memories. Depending upon one's religious tradition, clergy may ask for a volunteer to speak about the deceased at the funeral. As clergy devise their remarks, honesty should be the guide. Clergy may focus the funeral in such a way as to provide comfort and support, rather than just to promote correct theological viewpoints.

Clergy may mentally note those of the family that need special care based on what he or she observes. Clergy need to be involved with the survivors as early as possible after the death. Also, they must not see the funeral as the end of the need for caring or ministry, but as only one benchmark.

Too often, clergy drop by to visit the family once or twice after the funeral, maybe send a card or a book on grief, and feel their work with that family is done. This is not the case, and certainly is not all the ministry needed when a violent death has occurred. The grief process is much longer than we tend to realize. The grief process is often not only very long in cases of violent death, but is filled with landmines. The landmines are events in the criminal justice system which cause the survivors to have to relive their grief, time and time again. Time alone does not heal. In the next chapter we will look at the longterm needs of survivors and victims, the lengthy grief process, and suggest some practical steps for clergy response.

Chapter Three

Long Term Concerns

The following are statements by those who have lived them:

My wife was murdered in 1985. Her body was found in the Ocala National Forest after she had been missing for a week. She was shot twice in the head. For the first two years I was the prime suspect. During which, through rumors and people talking behind my back, my business was destroyed. After they finally caught the murderers, everybody said they were sorry. That's about it. My daughter was totally unable to deal with the trauma and has bad psychological problems because of it.* It happened at a tender age for her. She was only thirteen. We were all very close and she couldn't deal with it. She became increasingly difficult to handle, not drugs or anything like that. (Due to an altercation in which he acted to rescue his daughter from what he perceived as danger, he was arrested.) As a result [the authorities] took my daughter away. She has not lived at home for two years. She has been unable to live in foster homes. She has gone from foster home to foster home. She could not get along with her sister or get along with my parents and now ran away. . . . Now I'm not allowed to take care of my own daughter. All she wants to do is be home. She realizes now that there is no one like her father. She has one parent left . . .(*This daughter committed suicide in August, 1989)— a husband and father

I never thought my twenty-eight-year-old son would be murdered. My wife and I had never been arrested or gone to jail. We pay our taxes. I fought in WWII, and yet it happened. When it happens it presents a void that never goes away. You pick up the strings and carry on for the surviving relatives and offsprings. But you can never reconcile yourself to the one gnawing question that faces you, "Why me?" And I don't think there is an answer to it. . . . — a father

I suspected everybody. I went to every conceivable agency. From the F.B.I. to the F.D.L.E., to everybody to help and everything was a blank. . . . So I just turned around and launched my own investigation. I kept getting more involved in the investigation and coming up with loose ends which I was not educated enough to put together. I couldn't put the puzzle together. I found out this about this and about that. The only thing they [the police] could figure was for me to find this out was to have been the murderer myself. It was difficult to just mind your own business because that's the law.   *— A husband*

And people don't just grieve. There's a bitterness and rage they have. That something like that could be done to some- one they love. When a person dies a natural death, the hurt may be there, but I don't think the same bitterness or rage is. . . . It's hard for people to relate to us. The most com- mon thing I found from most people when you tell them a member of your family has been murdered is, "Why?" They can't imagine a person could be minding their own business and be murdered. They have to think you are doing some- thing bad or in to some criminal activity. They can't under- stand that it does happen to average people. And there is always a cloud over you. What were they doing? Were they drug dealers? Automatic! They assume they lived on the dark side of life. . . . The victimization never really ends.

The grief process for people dealing with a violent death is longer than other grief processes. While there are no "usual" lengths of time to move through the grief process, it should be noted that it is not unusual for two years to be necessary for the family to begin to stabilize. To reach a point where life can begin to be lived "normally" may take up to seven years. Initially, families are in a state of shock and disbelief. This is often followed by months of emotional numbness or depression. It is often during this time of depression that peo- ple, and clergy in particular, may expect the families to be get- ting on with their lives. The families or individuals involved may have unrealistic expectations of themselves as well. Pretending that everything is fine is very common behavior at this point. The truth is, a person or family that has experienced a violent death will never be the same again. This does not necessarily mean that they cannot put their lives back together in a different way, or still find purpose and satisfaction in living. However, it is a long-term process. If the murderer is arrested, there are also the landmines in the criminal justice system that must be dealt with in a realistic manner. There will be constant reminders of the loss of the loved one as survivors remember birthdays, anniversaries, special times and places, and so on. Therefore, for clergy to think that their ministry to survivors of a violent death is completed after a visit or call or two following the funeral is to ignore the reality of the situation. In some ways, the need for ministry is even greater as time goes on. Friends and companions expect survivors to be upset at the time of the tragedy or at the funeral, but six months or two years later they are not so understanding. Clergy need to be aware of survivors' needs and to develop a "care plan" to minister to the survivors of homicide.

Before designing a "care plan" it is important to identify some of the issues and needs of survivors of homicide.

Emotional Needs

A report on the first eighteen months of operation of the Victim Services Agency's' "Families of Homicide Victim's Project" in New York City, identified many of the emotions experienced by survivors and their families. *Anger* is one of the most common experiences. The feelings of anger are usually directed toward the person or persons thought responsible for the violent death. It is not uncommon at all for anger to be directed toward the police for not catching the murderers, or for not giving the family information on the investigation, or for insensitive treatment as perceived by the family. If the murderer or murderers are arrested, anger may be directed at the criminal justice system, and the officials involved, for lack of information, failure to notify them of hearings or trials, for plea bargaining with no explanations, for bond being granted the accused, confessions being thrown out, defense attorneys slandering the victim, too lenient a sentence if found guilty, for gain ("good") time in its many forms being granted to the convicted murderer — thereby reducing his or her sentence greatly, etc. The criminal justice system, from police, to the courts, and to the prisons, leaves much to be desired from the victim's family's perspective. In fact, survivors often feel anger to the degree that they feel they have experienced a "second victimization" by the system that they thought might bring some justice to bear.

Survivors often direct anger toward another family member because of imagined steps that that person might have taken to prevent the violent death. There are times when survivors direct anger at themselves for not being able to protect the one they loved. Anger is sometimes directed toward God. After all, how could God allow such a thing to happen? Survivors may feel anger because they have believed what someone, perhaps a clergy person, told them about it being "God's will." (It always surprises me when people say a violent death was God's will, as if they could read God's mind. For had it been anyone else but God, we would call such a being a criminal for willing such a violent act. The Scriptures reveal a God that wills good for God's people, not evil.)

Guilt is another emotion that many survivors experience. Sometimes this may be based in reality. It may be that the person feeling the guilt was negligent. More often than not, this guilt is based on an unrealistic idea that we can always protect our children or loved ones in a violent world. It may be guilt related to what the person wishes they had done based on hindsight, or that vague feeling that they should have known what was going to happen. Whether realistic or unrealistic, the feelings of guilt are strong and cannot be dismissed with a few words from clergy.

Sadness and *loneliness* are also powerful feelings. Often the survivors experience a depressed spirit, and a feeling of being left alone by the one who is deceased. There may even be unidentified anger at the deceased, making the person feel even more guilty and sad. Closely related, are feelings of *power-lessness* and *loss of control.* A person may also feel *isolated.*

Many victims or survivors feel *a loss of self-esteem,* a loss of self-worth. They feel *violated.* They may feel a sense of *meaninglessness,* a loss of purpose. Their lives have been shattered. The orderly world for them is broken. Things may not make much sense to them. They may have everything to live life with, but feel they have nothing to live life for. They may experience *suicidal thoughts or tendencies.* It is not uncommon for survivors to have visions of the deceased. The experience may seem to be very real. For some this is a comforting experience. For others, it is troubling and they feel they are "losing their minds." Emotionally, they may feel that they are on a roller coaster. For most there is a quiet *rage.*

It is difficult to overstate the intensity of these emotions in families of homicide victims. The acute state of grief may last two years. Friends and relatives of close survivors become uncomfortable after a while. They will admonish the survivors to get on with their lives. Oh! If they only could. When these admonishments don't work, friends and relatives tend to withdraw emotionally from the survivors. Thus, the situation is compounded by isolation and increased loneliness.

Physical Experiences

It is not uncommon for survivors and victim's family members to say that they have no energy. They feel tired, drained of emotional and physical strength. Psychosomatic ailments may appear or reappear. Stomach aches and headaches are common. It is as if they can not "stomach" what has happened, or the knowledge of what has happened "aches in their head."

Chest pains may also appear. Ulcers have been known to develop. There may appear a depression of the physical side of life. It is as though their very bodies are reacting against what has happened. Some people turn to a growing reliance on alcohol or drugs in an attempt to suppress the hurt and anguish. Insomnia may become a problem. They may feel that they can get no rest. When they do sleep, nightmares may haunt them.

It has been noted that many survivors or family members where a violent death has occurred seem to become accident-prone. Some people have speculated that this is due to constant distraction by thoughts of the tragedy; or due to a desire to punish themselves because they are alive and their loved one is not.

Family/Children Concerns

The surviving family members where a violent death has occurred often find their lives disrupted to a great degree. There may be a lack of communication following the death. People often don't know how to express feelings or emotions that follow such tragedy. When one reads about the emotions that are triggered by violent deaths, it is easy to see how communication can be disrupted. Feelings of alienation within the family may be great. Withdrawing from other family members is not uncommon. This may be caused by survivors not knowing what to say, not knowing if it is all right to feel and share these strong emotions, or trying to protect oneself from losing another person who is loved. There is also sometimes fear of adding to another's pain. Families often are torn with bitterness and the desire for revenge, as well as pressure from one or more family members to put the tragedy behind them. Parents may become overprotective of the remaining children. Children may be afraid to be away from the surviving parent, and fear that they may be "deserted" again. It is not unknown to have another member of the surviving family commit suicide on the birthdate or anniversary date of the deceased. It is a myth that tragedy and sorrow always draw families closer together.

Marital/Sexual Issues

Following violent death, husbands and wives may blame each other. The depression that follows often results in depressing any interest in sexual contact. There is the emotional pain stimulated by sexual contact. It is a reminder of the dead child and all the old hopes held for that child, from conception throughout pregnancy and beyond. Some couples try to rid themselves of the pain by divorcing the other parent of the dead child and starting over with someone new. There is an extremely high divorce rate for couples following the death of a child. Short of divorce, a couple may sell their home and move far away, so as not to be visually reminded of the past.

Job-Related Issues

Many survivors experience an inability to function or perform on the job. They have difficulty concentrating, they lose interest, or have little motivation. When they do work, it takes longer to accomplish the job than it did in the past. Many speak of feeling added pressures and stresses. Demotion and even loss of the job are not uncommon.

At the other extreme are those who run away from the pain by becoming work-aholics. They try to avoid the grief and the grieving spouse. Life and work are not the same.

Financial Concerns

Surviving families also face a number of financial concerns. While there are the obvious costs of the funeral, there may also be final medical expenses for the deceased. There may be medical expenses for health problems of other family members, including psychiatric care or counseling for surviving famly members. If the deceased was a "breadwinner" in the family, that income is lost forever. In some cases there are expenses for private investigators and/or private attorneys. Not only are there these expenses, but there may be other expenses that are indirectly related to the murder. For example, there may be the sister who gives up her college scholarship because she needs to be home with her family. Perhaps the family sells their home and moves because their child was killed in that home, and they are trying to get away from the memories. There may be a brother who has multiple one-car accidents because of his rage, self-destructive tendencies, or an inability to concentrate.

Religious/Spiritual Concerns

Many surviving individuals and families experience a loss of faith in God after such a great tragedy. Their loss of faith is sometimes compounded by guilt, because they feel their faith may not have been strong enough to sustain them. They may feel guilt and anger at God over what has happened.

The responses of clergy and their community of faith may force other issues. The responses, or expected responses and support from others in their church may be lacking, or may not be what was expected. Comments of clergy and members may communicate lack of understanding; the level of support may not be what survivors need.

The lack of expected responses by clergy and members of their community of faith, as well as the feeling that their faith was not strong enough, may shake the foundations of survivors' lives.

At the other extreme, the victim's family may be put on a pedestal by the clergy and community of faith, and praised for doing so well under the tragic circumstances, while all the time they feel that they are devastated, and not at all what people think. They may feel like imposters, and guilt may thus be increased.

Unfortunately, few clergy and even fewer congregations have received any training in how to respond to the tragedy of a violent death. People, even people of faith, feel uncomfortable and don't know what to say or do with those who have experienced such tragedy. Later, we will introduce some forms of ministry to victims of violent crime, as we explore in detail some of the spiritual crises that many victims experience.

Concerns From
Treatment by Professionals

The surviving families may have feelings of bitterness or hurt at the way various professionals have treated them during the tragedy. It is certainly not an easy job for police officers to have to inform a family of a violent death. Not all police officers have received any advice or training in this area.

Some may relate to family with brevity because of their own uneasiness. This may be interpreted by the family as a lack of caring. Hospital personnel are concerned with caring for the patient, and sensitivity to the family may, at times, not receive the attention it deserves. Hospital personnel may withhold information, and often correctly so, for the physician in charge to communicate the total picture accurately. Again, families may feel ignored or that the people involved do not care. Funeral directors may be interpreted by the family as "playing a role of sorrow." Clergy have been known to be insensitive in such situations. School counselors and teachers have usually had little or no training in helping the sibling of a murdered child. Even psychologists and psychiatrists may be somewhat unprepared to help families of violent crimes. The net result is frustration and anger on the part of the family who turned to the professionals to help them in this crisis only to find that the professionals were lacking.

Media Concerns

Often surviving families feel most hurt by the media people. Reporting of violent crimes can sometimes be inflammatory and slanderous. It has even been known to be inaccurate. Families feel that they are intruded on at funerals and other sensitive times. They may even feel exploited. This is particularly true when the coverage is prolonged. Worst of all is when the offender, the murderer, is apparently glorified or romanticized. Coverage may include the offender at various stages of the criminal justice system, while the victim and victim's family are not mentioned. Violent crime usually receives wide coverage. It often appears that we over-emphasize the violent criminal, while down-playing the victim and the devastation the violent criminal causes.

Legal and Judicial System
Issues and Concerns

Here is what victims have to say about the criminal justice system experience:

And the problem is the law has ceased to be a reflection of morality. It has started to become strictly maneuvering and legal loopholes. . . . There is right and there is wrong. Unfortunately, a lot of crimes are gotten away with based on loopholes and a lot of people are victimized based on loopholes. It's all legal . . . and it's time to stop it.

— a husband

It has been four years since my wife was murdered and now they are talking about appeals and going through the trial all over. And then you have to re-live the whole thing, with bloody clothes, and what you did last, and what she last said. The defense attorney trying to discredit you as a person, saying you are a bad person or you fought with your wife or you did this. It just keeps grinding away.

— a husband

Now, we found two young men. Both admitted to being there. They turned evidence on each other. One plea bargained for seventeen years, second degree murder. The other went to trial and he got the death penalty. I was at all the precedings prior to the trial. I was at all kinds of hearings where they tried to stop confessions and get all kinds of psychiatrists for them. I had to look at these people. What kind of people would do this and all the time the police were telling me very little. There were a lot of questions going through my mind as, what happened? Why did they do it? What went on? They even tried to imply that my daughter (age ten) was trying to prostitute herself. All this stuff was thrown on me. I had tremendous anger in me at the time. Anger and wondering what do I want to do. I wanted to kill these people. . . . It's five or six years later and where am I at?

I find that the guy who plea bargained for seventeen years to escape the death penalty and to escape a twenty-five-year mandatory and by the way charged with rape which they dropped. . . . I find out now he will be on the street next year. After only doing a little over six years. How do I feel about the criminal justice system? Very disappointed, because I heard a judge say seventeen years mandatory. . . . I am a victim. I go in there and the system has betrayed me. He is going to move in my neighborhood or near me. . . . He'll be walking in the shopping mall and who knows what he will do. I've had contact with his family. They are concerned about his welfare, that I don't go after him on the street. They even called me and said to me what are you going to do when he gets out? Why aren't they saying to me that they are really sorry about my daughter. . . . It bothers me. They know he did it. He admitted to it. He's guilty of murdering this little girl. They know how brutal the murder was. . . . Since I've been involved in the system I just can't believe.
                                                                      — a father

These three murderers were sentenced from five to fifteen years. Because of gain time they all walk today. . . . By behaving as normal people they got ten days a month off for each month they were sentenced. On a ten-year sentence they got 1200 days off before they even left the court room. They loose it only if they misbehave and then only the days for the month in which they misbehave. If they got a job in prison they get twenty days a month additional gain time each month and every month. There is even administrative gain time that can be an additional sixty days off for each month served. With jail overcrowding they can get days off. So much for truth in sentencing.

There are many issues that may arise in regard to the criminal justice system. Initially, these concerns will relate to the police. The fact that an arrest is not always made quickly or, sometimes, not at all, is a source of pain to the survivors. Strong emotions drive the survivors toward wanting to know who has committed the crime and toward wanting that person or persons arrested. There is frustration when this does not come to pass quickly. Some survivors have resorted to their own investigators or efforts. The danger is apparent. Police investigations can be jeopardized; the wrong person may be targeted for revenge by the survivor, and more tragedy can follow. Even if the guilty person is correctly identified and caught by the survivor, there is the danger of further destruction of the survivor's life if the survivor decides to act in vengeance. The survivor may be killed or end up in jail, too. For some survivors, the frustration is so great that they are willing to take such risks.

There are other related issues with the police. In some cases the survivors may be suspected by the police of being the perpetrators. Questioning and investigations by the police may raise these suspicions in the minds of other family members, friends, or business associates. This can quickly lead to isolation of the surviving victim, rude treatment by police and friends, and loss of business or job.

Another frustration can come from the police failing to provide information on the on-going investigation. In some cases there is no new information, in others it is necessary to keep the new information secret. Usually, the investigators will respond to questions and reassure the surviving victims that the investigation is continuing.

For people who have had little experience with the American justice system, the initial experience can shake the foundations of their faith. The system relates to survivors in ways that vary considerably from jurisdiction to jurisdiction. In Dade County, Florida, State's Attorney Janet Reno has led the way in developing openness and support for surviving victims of violent crime. Considerable effort is expanded in notifying survivors of hearings and trials, of helping them understand the process, of keeping them informed of the legal proceedings. Two members of the Miami Chapter of Parents of Murdered Children, Lisa Hardeman and Sara Arnwine, work in the State's Attorney's Office and assist families and victims of violent crime.

Unfortunately, this is not usually the case in most areas. Therefore, victims sometimes are not notified of hearings or trial dates. Victims do not know what to expect of the system and have little support.

Victims of violent crime are usually very upset when they find they cannot attend the trial. The law usually prevents anyone who is a witness in a case from sitting in the court during other testimony, so as not to confuse or alter their testimony. Many survivors find that if they are allowed in the court room, they may not show any emotion. Judges do not want the jury unduly influenced. They may be shocked to hear the defense attorney make various negative statements about their deceased loved one. They may find that they have little recourse or opportunity to refute such statements.

Victims are often shocked to realize what evidence is not allowed in court on the basis of what they consider minor technicalities. They may feel the prosecutor and police have mishandled the case.

They will find it amazing when confessions to the crime are thrown out of court with little or no explanation. The experience of plea bargaining with little explanation is also hard for survivors. By pleading to a lesser crime, the accused can obtain a lighter sentence.

If the accused is actually found guilty and a long sentence is handed down by the judge, the survivor may feel that justice is finally being done. This feeling is often short-lived. The victim will find that a long sentence is not necessarily what it appears to be. We need a "truth in sentencing" law. To encourage criminals to behave in jail, most states have a system often referred to as "gain time." Before a criminal even leaves the court room, up to one-third of the sentence has been reduced in order to encourage good behavior in prison. If a prisoner misbehaves, part of that reduced sentence may be added back to the time he or she must serve. It does not stop here. Additional time off the sentence will be granted if the prisoner attends high school or college classes or does other positive things. There may be, still, additional reductions of the original sentence, often carried out by the Corrections Department without any required approval by the judge in the case. Because of overcrowding in prisons, sentences are further reduced and people are released early to make room for new prisoners. In some states, convicted murderers are allowed out of prison on furlough. Parole is still practiced in some states. It is not uncommon for the family of the prisoner to be notified of the parole hearings while the family of the victims are not notified.

While it is necessary, perhaps, to offer incentives to prisoners to behave in prison and thus help protect correction officials who must work there, a person can not help but wonder at the lack of "truth in sentencing." A person sentenced to twenty-one years has an average of about seven years of the sentence reduced before leaving the court room. With all the other forms of gain time and early release, it is not impossible for the prisoner to leave the prison, not after twenty-one years but, perhaps, after only seven or eight years.

The experience of the survivor with the criminal justice system often leads to bitterness, a feeling that there is no justice. The system itself is often perceived as criminal. Unfortunately, the survivor's experience with the criminal justice system is not over. There are usually appeals and many times re-trial or re-sentencing. This process can go on for years. The survivor must re-live the tragedy each time. The grief process for surviving victims of violent crimes is full of these criminal justice land mines. Wounds are continually re-opened. Healing is therefore more difficult. There seems to be little closure. Sometimes while appeals are in process, the accused killer may be free on bail and living in the same neighborhood as the survivors of his or her victim.

Part of what happens to the surviving victims and family members is that when the criminal justice system interrupts the grief process, there is a shift away from grief to anger and resentment. The guilty person is perceived as less than human. Feelings of guilt, whether real or imaginary, in the surviving victims and family, are projected outward in anger.

Sometimes this temporarily relieves feelings of depression. Many times people shift back and forth between depression, anger, and resentment. The grief process continues in spite of the interruptions.

Long Term Concerns

Long Term Factors

- Emotional Needs
- Physical Experiences
- Family/Children Concerns
- Marital/Sexual Issues
- Job-Related Issues
- Financial Concerns
- Religious/Spiritual Concerns
- Treatment by Professionals
- Media Problems
- Criminal Justice Issues and Concerns

Survivors' Needs

- To continue in the grief process.
- Positive support from family, friends, and professionals, including clergy
- Reality orientation with many factors and concerns (see list above)
- Information on what to expect in the criminal justice system
- Professional help may be needed.

Chapter Four

Clergy in Response

S ome comments from victims:

> I would talk to someone like yourself, a clergyman, and they
> would give me the usual story. Let the justice system do it.
> Let God do it. They will get their reward in wherever. It's
> five or six years later and look what has happened.
>
> — a mother

> I wish the clergy would do the obvious job, in my opinion,
> they should be doing. They have a calling which is to help
> humanity, to help them believe in certain divine things and
> I think they come up short in the case of victims of violent
> crime, who need a kind word, a handshake, consolation from
> somebody who has some kind of an inward path toward the
> Supreme Being. It occurs to me that the majority of them,
> not all as you know, do their function at the funeral and in-
> terment, and if you are lucky, you might get a call . . . then
> it's a disappearing act. You never see them again and it is
> when you really need them as it begins to sink in what has
> really happened. That's when we need them and they are not
> there. They are off raising funds at bingo or whatever they
> do or doing their "happy" ceremonies, but there is another
> side to their function and I think they miss the boat. I don't
> think they can cope with it. They should learn more about
> the grief process and then, maybe, they would help more.
> But I don't even think they understand.   — a father

> The clergy is not trained for violent death. A person's reac-
> tion to violent death is completely different. I think they have
> to understand and help people deal with their rage and frus-
> tration, because it is the ultimate rape, and people don't just
> grieve. There is a bitterness and rage.   — a husband

At the end of the first chapter we presented a short list of "Dos and Don'ts" for clergy. There was no attempt to suggest a ministerial style for being with and helping people at a time of violent death. There was no attempt to present a theology of ministery, or concepts of psychology or counseling. It is assumed that most ministers will have dealt with basic psychology, counseling, and concepts and styles of ministry in college or seminary. There are many excellent books in these fields and no attempt to summarize or present one as the best guide for this context will be attempted. Instead, a brief outline of the grief process will be presented. The "ABCs" of grief intervention will be described. Each minister must respond to victims as himself or herself. Techniques are never enough. Clergy must resist the temptation to rely upon techniques and risk responding with the whole self. Each of us contains the treasure of God wrapped up in our "earthen vessel," that is, in ourself. Technique is not what it is about. Therefore, clergy must be him or herself and use the gifts that have been given by God.

Outline of Grief Process

The grief process has been described by many writers using various terms to describe stages of grief, phases of the grief process, and tasks faced within the grief process. The purpose of this short section is not to compare and contrast various theories or argue which is the most accurate or helpful. The bibliography will provide suggestions for additional exploration in detail. It seems that one helpful way to view the grief process is to think in terms of needs or tasks that the grieving person must face. William J. Warden in his book, *Grief Counseling and Grief Therapy*, provides a very detailed list of the books on grieving. Influenced by his identification of those tasks, I will list three basic tasks that each survivor must face.

First is the need for *evasion,* or the task of facing and accepting the loss. Many people experience the need to evade the reality of what has happened. Our bodies assist us to do this through shock, numbness, and denial. Our minds and bodies act defensively and allow us time to start adjusting to the new reality. Only when we are ready do we accept the new reality and loss. This is the first basic task in the grief process. Because this is the first step, other steps cannot be taken until this one has been completed.

The second follows the shock and disorganization of the first, namely the experience of disorganization in our life that follows the encounter with this new reality. Our need and task is to *experience the pain*. The experience of this pain comes in many feelings. Sadness, anger, guilt, yearning, fear, and anxiety are all part of the disorganization we experience. We need to experience the pain. To deny it, to mask it, is not the same as encountering it and facing it.

The third basic task is to *adjust to the new reality*, to re-invest our selves in life, to become reconciled. Our need is to become re-organized, to accept this terrible loss. This is the most difficult task for most people. It is not to pretend the loss never happened. It is not to go on with life as if it never happened. It is to truly re-organize life — and involves adjusting to changes in the family, in the physical environment, and in social arrangements. It involves accepting our memories, but not living in the past.

It means accepting the person who is missed, accepting a sense of emptiness or absence. For reconciliation and re-investment in life to occur, it also means realizing what is not lost or absent, finding what is good and positive. For many it calls for new roles or a shift in roles. It may call for developing new friends and, little by little, making new commitments. Reconciling feelings of anger and hostility are among the difficult tasks.

The grief process is a long process. People need time and cannot be hurried through it. Gradual progress is more the norm than sudden recovery. It is not always a consistent process of steady recovery. People need permission to backslide. Small goals or benchmarks are more helpful to people than the grand goal which always appears far off. Living one day at a time is a good rule of thumb.

The outcome of the grief process will not be a person exactly as they were before the tragedy. The person will not feel the same nor act the same as before. To expect them to be as before is unrealistic, and downplays the importance of what has happened and what the grieving person has felt.

The grief process can be seen as phases or tasks. The first phase is that of shock and disbelief, a need to evade this brutal new reality. The second phase is encounter with the new reality, the experience of disorganization with all of its emotional, physical, and spiritual distress. These feelings need to be experienced and encountered. The final phase is one of gradual recovery, of reconciliation and re-organization that faces the challenges and tasks of committing anew to life and to other people.

ABCs of Grief Intervention

The following is a very general guide for clergy who would intervene in the grief of another person. It is a guide of compassion. Compassion is "suffering with" another person. Clergy cannot expect to fully understand what a person in grief is experiencing, but this does not mean that a clergy person cannot intervene with compassion. It does mean that one does not intervene with thoughts that you have the answers or even a full understanding. Humility is required.

A — Acknowledge, Allow, and Accept

As clergy we must acknowledge our limitations. We must allow ourselves to be real human beings. We are more than the role we assume. We must accept who and what we are. Pretending will not do.

In intervening in the grief of another person, we must acknowledge that this is a person who has a right to their feelings

— even if those feelings alarm or even shock us. Unless we acknowledge this person as a person with rights to their own feelings, we will try to manipulate them according to our own desires and fears. We will need to acknowledge the fears, worries, and unresolved concerns that are within us, and which are made conscious by relating to a surviving victim or family. Our fear of our own death and suffering will need to be faced in order for us to effectively minister. Our basic beliefs and our concern about God's goodness and justice will be unavoidable. Fears that such a tragedy could strike our family will also be there. Other issues related to the above may surface. It may be helpful to keep an informal journal or notebook and write down our own fears and doubts, and to keep track of other feelings and issues which arise.

The first step in dealing with these limitations is to acknowledge that we have them. If we deny them, we may find ourselves struggling with them when we think we are ministering to others. Our own feelings and fears may get in the way of real ministry. Instead of focusing on the victims, we may end up focusing on ourselves. Our judgment will be misdirected, our help diluted.

We need to allow for our humanity. We will not be able to help everyone. We do not always choose the best words or actions. We may not always be our best self. We need to acknowledge and to allow ourselves to be human. When our own feelings swell up within us as we minister to victims of violent crime, we must allow ourselves to feel. We must allow ourselves time to deal with these troubling feelings. To deny them will help no one, and may get in everyone's way.

As clergy we also need to allow the people to whom we would minister to be human. We cannot expect them to act consistently with the highest principles of our faith. There may be times when they say or do things totally at odds with our views of the faith. We need to allow them to experience their grief and anger, and the other emotions that follow tragedy. We must resist our own need to have them respond in perfect faith, or to respond as we would want them to respond. We must allow them to be themselves. We must allow God to be God. We need to allow for the fact that they may experience many ups and downs. They will probably never be the same person they were before the tragedy.

We need to accept people and ourselves as we are. Wishful thinking will not change either, nor will it change the painful situation in which we have been called to minister.

B — Be There

To be in ministry, to be supportive, and to be involved means clergy must be there with the person. While there is no substitute for the clergy's presence, in long term care, use of the telephone can be authentic. A telephone call, particularly on birthdays, death date, or holidays can mean a lot to a person. Clergy are busy, and the telephone can be an instrument of ministry. Of course, the telephone is not a substitute for one's presence. After the funeral, people tend not to follow up with support to survivors. Clergy can develop a systematic plan to be there for victims. The Reverend Donald Norris, pastor of the First Baptist Church of South Miami, has offered one such model. It is based on a "Chaplain's Care Plan" used by Rev. Norris at Jackson Memorial Hospital, Miami.

The plan can take the form of a single piece of paper. On one side basic information (such as name, address, and phone number) is recorded. Under the heading "General Observations" notes might be made about what happened. The tragedy need not be described in great detail. Under the headlines "Background," notes might be made concerning social, economic, educational, social, and familial situation. Under the heading "Religious History," notes could be made about the person's faith stance and faith issues. Under the heading "Emotions and Personality," the clergy using the plan could make notes depending upon his or her training as to a subjective assessment of the individual characteristics or issues. Thus, on one side of the page, one has an objective and subjective identification of the person and the particular situation. On the backside or page two, under the heading "Pastoral Care Needs," one can list the particular needs that have been identified. Among such needs may be any of those identified in Chapter One or Two, but stated specifically. For example, one might observe that the person is struggling with a real or unreal sense of guilt. Perhaps the need to be addressed is loss of self-esteem, loss of meaning and purpose, or depression, anger, or suicidal thoughts.

There may be other needs that are more obvious, such as financial issues or job-related issues. The summaries in Chapters One and Two identifying many of the needs or concerns of surviving victims and families can stimulate awareness.

Under the heading "Pastoral Goals," short-term and long-term goals can be identified. A short-term goal might be to help that person acknowledge their anger and loss of control. Another short- and/or long-term goal might be to help activate a support group of family and friends for the survivor. Examples of other goals might be to connect the survivor to an on-going professional support group, to help the person understand the criminal justice system, to help the person understand the grief process, and to help the person deal with depression and the sense of loss of power or control. The goals should be directly related to the needs identified above.

To have goals is never enough. Under the heading "Pastoral Care Objectives," one should identify how you will reach the goal. For example, to link the person with a support group: "I will take the person to a group meeting of Parents of Murdered Children with me on February 14th." To help the person acknowledge their anger; "I will visit him/her at home on February 2nd. The visit will be to encourage the expression of his anger and help him/her see it is all right to be angry." There should be an objective that is precisely stated to go with each goal.

I would also suggest that the clergy develop a monthly calendar of birthdates, death dates, anniversaries, court hearings, trials, and other important dates for each person. A master calendar containing all such dates could then be used

Pastoral Care Plan

I.   Name   _____

       Address   _____

       _____

II.   General Observations   _____

       _____

       _____

III. Background   _____

       _____

       _____

       _____

IV.   Religious History _____

       _____

       _____

       _____

V.   Emotions and Personality _____

       _____

       _____

       _____

       _____

— Side 2 —

VI. Pastoral Care Needs _____

_____

_____

VII. Pastoral Care Goals
     A. Short-term _____

     _____

     _____

     _____

     _____

     B. Long-term _____

     _____

     _____

     _____

     _____

VIII. Pastoral Care Objective/Actions _____

     _____

     _____

     _____

IX. Special Dates:

     Death Date _____

     Birth Date _____

     Anniversary: _____

     Court Dates: _____

to help the clergy to make a telephone call, or visit these victims on crucial dates. Relying upon individual care plan sheets is usually unsatisfactory. Without such a master calendar, things will be overlooked. Such care plan sheets are vital in organizing and planning systematic follow-up care for people with a great need. The individual sheet should be reviewed before each telephone call or visit. Notes can be made after each call or visit. I do not believe notes should be made during the call or visit as it distracts one from truly focusing on the person and relationship. Paper work and records should be helpful, not get in the way. The obvious advantage of using such a form, or modified form, is that systematic follow-up care can be planned. Important needs and plans will not be easily overlooked or forgotten.

C — Care, Care, Care

What matters most is care. Compassion. Techniques and forms make little difference unless care is part of the pastoral relationship. Clergy must be fully human and dare to act out of that humanity. People who have experienced a violent tragedy are not usually looking for theological critiques of faith, or theological discussions whatever questions they may ask. They are seeking sympathy, compassion, and caring. There will be time for theological questions and discussions as time goes on. Clergy who respond with care and compassion above all else will be ministering, and their mistakes will be over-looked by those in need.

Responding to Spiritual Issues

As part of long-term follow-up care, the time will come when clergy will be appropriate in responding to questions with theological reasoning. There is no firm guide to determining this point. Even when clergy feel the point is at hand, care should be given to offering theological reasoning within the expression of care and compassion. It should be made clear that one may have difficulty in accepting the theological reasoning offered, and that one does not have to accept the reasoning to be loved by God or to be accepted by you as a clergy person. Remember that all that is said is very personal to the victim, and guilt and anger at God are usually present. Sometimes, we clergy place an even greater burden on victims by our approach to theological reasoning as it relates to God, suffering, and death.

Consider some of the spiritual issues and concerns that may be encountered. Many people believe it is God's will no matter what happens. If tragedy strikes, then it is God's will. If your child is murdered, it is God's will. If it was anyone other than God who willed it, we would call them a murderer. The obvious response is to be angry with God if you believe God willed the murder of your child. It should be clear that I don't believe it is God's will for such evil to happen. Usually, if a person believes it is God's will, then they are angry at God, the source of their life. They become alienated from God and from life. Or, they feel that if it was God's will, then it must be that God is punishing them. They, not being perfect, can usually find some reason why God should punish them. They haven't been going regularly to church or synagogue, or they haven't been tithing, or some other reason. They may, then, feel guilty for bringing on the tragedy by their act or failure to do whatever they feel they should have been doing. The anger may be aimed at God for such a harsh and unjust punishment or aimed at themself for "causing" the tragedy. This self-hate can lead to depression and self-alienation, as well as tremendous guilt. My understanding of God and Scripture lead me to reject God willing evil on God's people. This is a theological issue that has tremendous emotional consequences. I believe we must help each person from our own faith perspective understand that God is not evil and that God does not will evil on God's people.

A second spiritual issue is related. If we understand that God does not will evil and that murder is not God's will, then we must deal with the question of why God allows it to happen. Isn't God a loving God? Isn't God a just God? Many people feel that if God allows such terrible things to happen, then God doesn't love them. If God doesn't intervene, then God is allowing terrible injustice and is not a God they want to worship or have anything to do with again.

Perhaps, the most honest response is to acknowledge that we do not know why such things happen or are allowed. We sometimes say that God must be able to weave all these things together in God's grand design. All of this challenges our view of God as being good and all powerful. Does it mean God is not good? That God is not all powerful?

My personal view is that God is good and all powerful. I believe, however, that God truly loves us and has given us the gift of human freedom. This means that we can choose to love God and to cooperate with God's purposes, or refuse. God has shown God's love for us by refusing to force us to be and to do good. God refuses to intervene even when we are making wrong or evil choices. God does not save us from the consequences of our actions, but allows us true human freedom. God has limited himself as an act of love, so that we can have human freedom. Much of the hurt, tragedy, and pain in this world is the result of our wrong choices and misuses of human freedom. Because of our misuse of human freedom, our revolt against God, God suffers. Therefore, what seems to be an act of injustice or lack of goodness or love on God's part, is actually an act of God's love. Without human freedom we would be slaves, or robots, and not human — and certainly not beings in God's image. Our misuse of human freedom brings tragedy upon ourselves and pain to God by rejection of God's Way of living. Such theological reasoning is not helpful to people caught up in the pain of tragedy. Perhaps, such theological explorations need to take place in our churches and synagogues when tragedy is not upon us. It would help other good people to understand that tragedy is not necessarily God's punishment nor our excuse to avoid or join in blaming the victims.

Some might ask if God performs miracles, a form of intervention. The Scriptures certainly contain accounts of such intervention. The surprising thing to me is that while Jesus performed miracles he often told people not to tell others. In fact, many seemed to follow him because of the miracles, but got so caught up in these signs that they would not hear the message he brought. At any rate, the miracles seem to be done with a purpose of pointing to Jesus' ministry as the work of God.

I believe a deeper demonstration of God's love toward us is seen in the laws of nature that God has put into motion. It is only because God's laws of nature give us an orderly universe that we can use our human freedom. Without an orderly universe, our human freedom would be of little use. If God acted anyway God chose to act in the world, our human freedom would be undercut. Therefore, hurricanes, earthquakes, tornados, lightning, and other disasters are not God's direct will, but the consequence of the laws of nature. Disease and infections would have to be considered part of nature, too. In our human freedom, and as stewards of the earth, we can exercise certain control over nature. I do not believe God wills cancer or any other disease or illness on us.

A third spiritual issue is prayer. When we pray, I believe we can express to God our deepest feelings, hopes, and desires. We can ask God to strengthen and to help a person who is ill, or the victim of tragedy. We can express our hope that God will save the person or make the person whole. I believe we should also realize that we cannot expect God to re-order the universe at our request, and then get angry or drop-kick our faith when God does not do *our* will.

We may need to accept reality, to accept the universe as God has ordered it. Again, I believe these insights and issues are best addressed when tragedy is not upon us. When tragedy strikes, we need care and compassion — not theological critiques.

Writing from within my own Christian tradition, I believe there is a theological insight that is valid in and without tragedy. The Christian faith proclaims a God who suffers. In particular, we proclaim a God who in Jesus Christ was tempted as we are, and who suffered and died for us on the Cross. The God of the Christian faith is not just a creator God who ordered the universe, gave human beings freedom, and went off somewhere. We proclaim a God who has entered into our experience of life, who knows what it is to be human, to suffer, and to die. We proclaim a God of compassion, who truly cares and who suffers with and for us. In Jesus we proclaim a God who knows about violent death, a God who is himself the parent of a murdered son. I believe it is important that we share this aspect of a God who suffers with those who suffer. God knows and shares our tragedy, and is a source of help in times of trouble. In being with the Miami Chapter of Parents of Murdered Children, I have seen what a difference it makes for people to share with others who truly know what they have experienced and who are currently enduring. I believe we need to share the understanding of a God who suffers and who can understand others who suffer.

There are other spiritual problems beyond basic questions. A fourth spiritual issue is the issue of sharing, of being part of a community. Tragedy pushes people toward isolation. The community of faith needs to take the initiative to keep the victim part of the community, or to bring them back into the community. To do this, the community of faith needs to seriously be challenged and taught to understand their own identity. If they are a community of faith, a people of God, then they must explore who they are and the nature of their ministry or work. If they are part of the family of God, then they need to grow in being a family and in building close relationships. Most churches and synagogues have a long way to go to be all they should be. A serious study and discussion of one's identity and purpose is a good place to start. The development of small groups, particularly of support groups, would be an excellent step. These support groups could be trained by clergy and other professionals, perhaps, within the particular church or synagogue, in how to be supportive to individuals and families who experience tragedy or are in crisis. Such groups are not a substitute for clergy, but an extention of the community of faith's support and ministry. There are plenty of people with needs. Those who participate learn and grow. People who have experienced a tragedy can help and be helped by serving, and using their tragedy to help others. Help and guidance may be obtained in developing your support group from local Parents of Murdered Children chapters, Compassionate Friends, Parents Grief Support Groups at local hospitals, Hospice groups, Mothers Against Drunk Driving, or other groups that specialize in grief support work.

People who experience grief through violent death need to be involved in community and not be isolated by the tragedy. Becoming involved in churches or synagogues again may not be easy. Clergy may need to hold their hand and help ease their way. By helping the community of faith understand tragedy and theological ways of understanding it, re-entry can be eased for victims. Understanding, acceptance, and support need to be generated.

Victims will never be the way they were before the tragedy. Realistic expectations should be encouraged. Remember, no one likes to hear the stories of tragedy when it makes them realize it could happen to them. Most people don't want to be depressed. Building a loving, supportive, and understanding group within the community of faith can make a difference and can help the whole community.

A fifth spiritual problem, meaning and purpose in life, requires more than a general discussion of one's philosophy of live. Surviving victims find it difficult to re-invest themselves into life. What once was meaningful may seem shallow. Helping the survivors explore meaning and purpose in their own life is difficult. Viktor Frankl has suggested that people help create meaning and purpose by what they give to life, what they take from life, and how they face the ultimate situations of guilt, suffering, and death. Frankl's books *Psychotherapy and Existentialism, The Will to Meaning,* and *The Unheard Cry for Meaning* may be of interest to clergy. A. J. Ungersma's *The Search For Meaning* and Joseph Fabry's *The Pursuit of*

Meaning also offer valuable insights. The particular teachings of one's faith tradition can be shared with the survivor. It is important to remember that each person must work out their own understanding. It is not something that can be imposed. It is also important to remember that one's sense of meaning and purpose is not just an intellectual commitment, but also emotion. This journey of faith involves putting the tragedy in the larger context of a faith stance. Very basic questions must be asked, such as, what do I really believe? What is the nature of human life? What is death? What, if anything, lies beyond? It is a slow, on-going process in which clergy can be very helpful.

A sixth spiritual issue is found in anger, hatred, and the issue of forgiveness. For many victims these strong emotions and feelings are overwhelming. They may feel these emotions are at odds with their sense of spiritual identity and with the teachings of their faith. Many clergy are uncomfortable with such emotions. The temptation is for clergy to tell the surviving victim that they must forgive the person or persons who have committed this violent crime. This is a message that victims are not able to hear or respond to early in the grief process. To expect them to do so may be expecting the impossible. In fact, clergy may be putting a heavy burden of guilt upon the victims when they are unable to forgive. Victims will become even more alienated from God, and angry at all connected with God. I have known of only one case where forgiveness was possible early in the grief process. Suezann, the daughter of a Church of The Brethren minister, the Rev. Bill Bosler, saw her father stabbed to death in the church parsonage a few days before Christmas. She, too, was stabbed and left for dead. But she was able to ask that the murderer not receive the death penalty. She certainly did not want the murderer back on the streets, but because of her father's views against the death penalty, she spoke on behalf of the murderer.

In most cases, the anger will remain. Only after much time can the surviving victims rechannel that anger into positive efforts, such as work with other surviving victims or in efforts to reform the criminal justice system. Perhaps, this is the most positive direction in which clergy can help to lead victims. The anger remains. Anger, directed toward a good purpose, can be a powerful motivation. The ability to forgive is something no one can be talked into. Forgiveness and the ability to forgive originates from God.

In my experience as a Christian minister, I have observed much misuse of Scripture. How often do we quote Jesus in Matthew 5:43-48 about loving our enemies? When victims fail to show the aspect of love of enemies we expect, we judge them as being unchristian. We might do well to look at the context in which Jesus spoke. It appears that Jesus was calling people to mature ways of responding in day-to-day life. He was calling people not to just love those who loved them, but to initiate a life of reconciliation by reaching out to others. He was encouraging us to act beyond simple self-interest. I hope murder is not yet seen as a day-to-day activity. Both the Old and New Testaments strongly condemned murder beyond other crimes. Murder was a supreme act against God. Rather than expect the victims or the community to forgive, the Old Testament called for purging the evil from the midst of the community. (Deuteronomy 13:5) The underlying concept was that society was in covenant with God. Murder broke the covenant. To repair the broken relationship, the evil had to be purged. The crime of murder undermined the existence of the community with God, and treated God's graciousness with indifference, turning a community's oath of loyalty to God into a lie. The crime of murder was an attack on God. Capitol punishment was socially sanctioned. (Exodus 21:2, Deuteronomy 27:24, Leviticus 24:17) Capitol punishment was the punishment for a long list of crimes besides murder. Most of us today would not support capitol punishment for profaning the Sabbath, (Exodus 31:14), adultery (Leviticus 20:10), blaspheming the Holy Name (Leviticus 24:16), contempt for certain judiciary decisions (Deuteronomy 17:8-13), false prophecy (Deuteronomy 18:20), and certain other crimes. In the New

Testament the death penalty was never challenged, even when it was applied to Jesus. Jesus was officially charged with violation of the public order (Matthew 27:38) and sedition (Matthew 14:10) as was John the Baptizer. Jesus said he came not to abolish the law and prophets but to fulfill them. Jesus quoted the law and often followed with an even more demanding interpretation than had been previously accepted. He said not only do not kill, but don't even be angry with your neighbor.

While the death penalty was practiced and accepted in ancient Israel, it was based on theological reasoning and within a context of a covenant society. Today, we live in a secular society that distinguishes between church and state. A direct application of the practices reported in Scripture to a secular society may not be possible or theologically sound. I might add that the testimony of two eye witnesses was usually required for conviction and execution in biblical times. At one point the eye witness who testified had to actually initiate the process of execution. Stoning was the most common method, but burning and beheading were also used.

Vengeance was not acceptable. In Deuteronomy 32:35 where God says, "Vengeance is mine . . .", it originally meant that God would act against foreign powers. In Romans 12:14-19, Paul applies the concept to everyday life. Even the much quoted "eye for an eye" (Leviticus 24:20) passage was not originally support for revenge, but rather intended to limit excessive revenge. It was meant to limit feuds and blood revenge. Even executions in biblical days were not to satisfy the demands of the victim's family or to act as a deterrence. It was understood that God was making the demand to restore the covenant.

These are six of the most common spiritual issues. Implied in all of them is the question, Is there really a God? There are spiritual dimensions to all the needs and issues cited in these chapters. The scope of this short book makes it impossible to address them all.

Some Concluding Notes

Clergy want to help. The problem is, we don't always know what to do or what to say. In the situations described in this book, there is not much we can say or do that will make things any worse than they already are.

Clergy need to be with the person rather than trying to solve the problem. There is a big difference. It is the difference between being people-centered and task-oriented. Clergy will not solve the problem; God will do the healing. Clergy can enable the healing process by being with the person and providing supportive help.

All of us think we know how to hear and to listen. It is important to hear people's feelings, not just the content of their words. The focus throughout this book is that clergy need to respond from the heart with care instead of from the mind with words or intellectual reasoning. Respond first to the person's feelings, and then to their thoughts, ideas, or actions. Focus on the meaning, on what the person is saying about him or herself.

Clergy can *respond*, not just *react* to people. Reactions suggest an unthinking or uncritical action. To be helpful, clergy need to be aware of their own feelings in the situation and not simply react with those feelings. Instead, respond. Respond with an appropriate response that focuses on the other person rather than on one's own feelings.

It is not uncommon for surviving victims to be in conflict within. Clergy need to be able to hear and to identify that conflict without taking sides. Sometimes, helping the person recognize the conflict can help the person to work through to a resolution. A sure sign of conflict is the strong asserting of a point or issue. Usually, the person is trying to convince himself or herself of that same point. Clergy can best help by accepting the conflict, the pain, the anger, and even the sin in the other person. Condemning cuts off dialogue. In fact, the more we attempt to teach the person how to grow or how to overcome the tragedy, the more resistance we will encounter.

Clergy in Response

Clergy Do's

- Become familiar with the grief process.
- Realize each person handles grief in their own way.
- Know the grief process is a guide not a detailed chart.
- Acknowledge, allow, and accept.
- Be there, be supportive, be involved.
- Care, care, care.
- Adapt and use a pastoral care plan.
- Respond to spiritual problems.
- Be sensitive to the emotional implications of faith affirmations.
- Be committed for long-term.
- Be with the person. Don't try to "solve" the problem.
- Respond to the person's feelings, don't just react.
- Listen to feelings, not just the content of words.

Clergy Don'ts

- Don't expect every person to go through grief the same as others.
- Don't force theological explanations on grieving persons.
- Don't think intellectual explanations solve emotional pain.
- Don't confuse your needs with those of the victim.
- Don't impose your expectations on victims.
- Don't say you understand.

Common Spiritual Issues and Questions

- Is there really a God?
- Is this tragedy God's will?
- If God is good, why did God allow this tragedy?
- Is God punishing me (or my family)?
- If God is all powerful, why did God not intervene?
- Does God know my pain and can God help?
- If God is just, why did God allow this tragedy?
- Why didn't God answer my prayer?
- How can I ever worship God or be part of the church again?
- Is there any meaning or purpose to life? (to my life?)
- Will God punish me for being so angry at God and the murderer?
- Can God still accept and forgive me, while I can not forgive the murderer?
- Is it wrong to want revenge?
- Is there really life after death?
- Spiritual dimensions to all needs and issues.

As clergy, we may discover that what we don't like in the other person is a reflection of something we don't like in ourselves. Some behavior we object to may really be a sign of defense by the person to a real or imagined threat. We need to learn to recognize it for what it is, and not let it get in the way of our relationship with the person.

As clergy, we have often been taught to be "nice." Being nice and trying always to cheer up others are ways of discounting the feelings of others. It suggests that we do not take seriously the feelings, the pain of the other person. It suggests that we do not take seriously the irritating and demanding behavior that is a mask for that pain.

To truly help others we must face our own spiritual poverty and humbly share our presence with that person whom we seek to help.

Chapter Five

Taking Care
of the Caregiver

Many clergy are truly givers. We tend to be what Carl Jung called "extraverts." We are outer-directed and expend much of our energy toward others and toward trying to improve the world. There are times when an enemy imbalance develops. We become "burnt-out." Since we tend to be the idealists, the optimists, the good boys or girls, and the ones who assume a parent role, we can become not only burnt-out but also resentful. We tend to believe that the way to serve God and to experience love is in giving and relating to others. Sometimes our energy runs out and we refuse to face that fact. As givers, we expend energy by our work, by trying to change people, by talking, by trying to be in control, and by having high expectations of others. We have difficulty receiving. We prefer to be giving. We are uncomfortable pampering ourselves or even taking care of ourselves. We become resentful when we can't be in our role of giver or when people don't seem to appreciate all that we do. The basic truth is that we need a balance in our lives between giving and taking. We cannot really be good givers unless we also learn to take care of ourselves.

We need to take care of the caregiver. In order to survive in such energy-draining work, we need to take some concrete steps to nurture and protect ourselves:

1. Recognize our humanity.
2. Recognize our limitations.
3. Be enablers, not magicians or super-problem solvers.

4. Take a day off.
5. Find a quiet spot and use it.
6. Take time in which we do nothing.
7. Get more sleep.
8. Accept praise, encouragement, support, and help.
9. Let others help and do things.
10. Change our routine occasionally.
11. Spend time with our spouse and our children.
12. Express our helplessness and frustration.
13. Focus on good things, not just bad.
14. Pamper ourselves.
15. Talk with a friend. Develop a buddy system, a support group for ourselves.
16. Learn to say "No."
17. Laugh!
18. Play!
19. Be a resource to ourselves. Explore!
20. Say "I choose" rather than "I should."

You are important. If you are burnt-out, stressed out, in the hospital ill, what good can you do? If you learn to take as well as give, your life will be more balanced. You will be a better self.

We usually speak of God's work and our call to be part of that work. We might recognize that a major part of God's work is "people making." What kind of people are we if we do not attend to this part of God's work?

Additonal Reading and Resources

General:

American Association of Suicidology: 2459 S. Ash St., Denver, CO 80222.

Baugher, Robert, Calija, Marc. *A Guide for the Survivor Who Has Lost a Loved One Through a Sudden Death,* Campus Box 902, Peabody College, Nashville, TN 37203.

Colgrove, Bloomfield & McWilliams. *How to Survive the Loss of a Love.* Bantam, 1977.

Cain, Albert C. *Survivors of Suicide,* Springfield, Illinois: Charles C. Thomas, 1972.

Foglia, Barbara Bell. "Survivor—Victims of Suicide," 1967.

Grollman, Earl A. *Concerning Death: A Practical Guide for the Living,* Boston: Beacon Press, 1974.

Grollman, Earl A. *Living When a Loved One Has Died,* Beacon Press, 1977.

Jackson, Edgar. *Understanding Grief,* Abingdon Press, 1951.

Jackson, Edgar. *You and Your Grief,* Channell Press, 1961.

Kushner, Harold S. *When Bad Things Happen to Good People,* Schoeken Books, 1981.

LeShan, Edna. *Learning to Say Good-Bye When a Parent Dies,* MacMillan Publishing Co., 1976.

Manning, Doug. *Don't Take My Grief Away from Me,* Creative Marketing, P.O. Box 2423, Springfield, IL 62705.

Miller, William A. *When Going to Pieces Holds You Together,* Augsburg, 1976.

Rubin, Theodore. *The Angry Book,* Collier Books: New York, 1969.

Suicide Information Center: 6377 Lake Apopka Place, San Diego, CA 92119.

Westberg, Granger. *Good Grief,* Fortress Press, 1976.

Counsellors, Clergy, Caregivers, Support Persons:

Bergman, A. "Psychological Aspects of Sudden Unexpected Death in Infants and Children," Pediatric Clinics of North America, Vol. 21, Feb. 1974, pp. 115-121.

Grollman, Earl. *Suicide: Prevention, Intervention, Postvention,* Boston: Beacon Press, 1971.

Henry, Andrew F. and James F. Short, Jr. *Suicide and Homicide,* Glencoe, IL: Free Press, 1954.

Hoff, Lee Ann, *People in Crisis: Understanding & Helping*, 1978.

Johnson, Paul. *Psychology of Pastoral Care,* New York and Nashville: Abingdon Press, 1953.

Kliman, Ann S. *Crisis: Psychological First Aid,* 1978.

O'Connor, Ph.D. *Letting Go With Love: The Grieving Process,* La Mariposa Press, Apache Junction, AZ, 1984.

Parkes, C. M. & Weiss, *Recovery From Grief,* Basic Books, New York, 1983.

Rando, Theresa A., *Grief, Dying, and Death*, Research Press: Champaign, Illinois, 1984.

Ross, Eleanora. "Suicide and the Stages of Grief," *Death Education,* Vol. 2, No. 4, Winter 1979.

Schuyler, Dean. "Counseling Suicide Survivors: Issues and Answers," *Omega,* Vol. 4, No. 4, 1973.

Shneidman, Edwin. *Suicidology: Contemporary Developments,* 1976, 76-7031.

Stone, Howard. Crisis Counseling, 1976.

Stone, Howard. *Suicide and Grief,* Philadelphia: Fortress Press, 1972.

Bereaved Parents:

Alvarez, A. *The Savage God,* New York: Random House, 1972.

Giovacchini, Peter. *The Urge to Die: Why Young People Commit Suicide,* New York: MacMillan, 1981.

Klagsbrun, Francine. *Too Young to Die,* New York: Pocket Books, 1981.

Schiff, Harriet Sarnoff. *The Bereaved Parent,* Crown Publishers, Inc., 1977.

Vonnegut, Mark. *The Eden Express,* New York: Praeger, 1975.

Organizations That Provide Information:

American Association of Suicidology, Central Office, 2459 S. Ash, Denver, CO 80222.

Clergy-in-Service Training Initiative, P.O. Box 163304, Sacramento, CA 95816

Homicide Survivor Group, Inc., P.O. Box 6201, Clearwater, FL 34618.

The Institute for Studies of Self Destructive Behaviors and The Suicide Prevention Center, 1041 S. Menio St., Los angeles, CA 90006.

Merck, Sharp and Dohme, Health Information Services, West Point, PA 19486.

National Institute of Mental Health, Mental Health Emergencies Section, 5600 Fishers Lane, Rockville, MD 20852.

Parents of Murdered Children, Miami, P.O. Box 5512, Hialeah, FL 33014

Parents of Murdered Children, National Office, 100 E. 8th St., Room B-41, Cincinnati, OH 45202.

Suicide Prevention Center, Inc., 184 Salem Avenue, Dayton, OH 45406.

Suicide Information Center, 6377 Lake Apopka Place, San Diego, CA 92119.

DATE DUE